DOG FASHION

haute couture for your hound

SUSIE GREEN

CICO BOOKS

LONDON NEW YORK

First published in 2007 by CICO Books
an imprint of Ryland Peters & Small
519 Broadway, 5th Floor, New York, NY 10012

10 9 8 7 6 5 4 3 2 1

A CIP catalog record for this book is available from the Library of Congress

ISBN-13: 978 1 906094 13 3
ISBN-10: 1 906094 13 6

Printed in China

Editor: Kesta Desmond
Designer: David Fordham
Photographer: Lucinda Symons

CONTENTS

AT HOME

For dogs, just like people, home is where the heart is. Home is where a dog can really be herself and know that she is truly loved and can give love in return. She knows you don't mind if she chills out on the couch in little more than a collar, or clambers onto that comfy velvet chair. "Down!" is just a word, not a command, when she's with her family.

Home is also where the fashion-conscious pooch keeps her stylish wardrobe, does her personal grooming, and gets herself ready to take on the world with you by her side. And home is where the sociable dog entertains her friends...

LEFT: *This gorgeous lime-green collar with silver bone detail complements Wallis the Weimaraner's coat and eyes beautifully.*

ENTERTAINING

Every dog likes to entertain. It's a desire that goes back to the days when dogs lived in packs and used to share dinner. Nowadays, to the regret of many canines, meals are less likely to be venison than dry cookies. Still, when having buddies over, there's a whole host of delicious new delicacies that their doggy ancestors could never have dreamed of: beef-flavored sponge cake, carob minty mints and peanut butter cups to name but a few.

Lily, following in the pawprints of the modish Victorian canine, always sends out engraved invitation cards. She finds texts and emails far too casual.

One of the things Lily likes most about entertaining chez-elle is that it allows her to set the style of dress. So if Lily has just purchased a pristine flowered suit, all the other dogs on the block have to turn up smart-casual. But if Lily's latest acquisition is a cool red T-shirt, then it's street style for all.

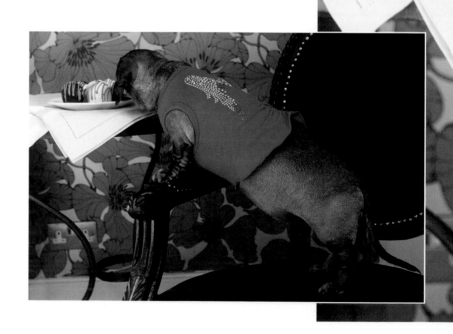

RIGHT: *Here Lily models her latest casual yet glitzy outfit—a red top with a motif of glittering gold wings that accentuate her own fur tones. Ever the conscientious hostess, Lily is making absolutely sure that the cakes really are fit for canine consumption.*

CHILLING OUT

Home is for chilling out and for living your dreams. And this trio of Great Danes do both in style. When they're not patrolling the grounds of their spacious estate or taking a relaxing dip in the swimming pool, they like to lounge on the couch watching television. Recently they have been watching *Ugly Betty*, but their long-term favorites are *Superman* and repeats of *The Godfather*, with *The Sopranos* coming a close third. They also enjoy royal watching.

LEFT: *Digby stretches out languidly while considering whether to take a stroll around the grounds.*

BELOW: *Dylan, Digby, and Boris show disdain for traditional leather collars and new-fangled bling alike. Simple but striking bandanas are their idea of cool.*

BATH TIME

City canines, like city people, are subject to the dirt that pollutes the air of all the world's great metropolises. Our hair gets dirty, we feel the grime of the city on our faces, and so do our dogs.

Now if Poppy and Loulou go for a romp in the mud, they don't mind missing a shower, but after a morning shopping in downtown Manhattan or London's Bond Street, it's a completely different story. They just can't wait to jump in the tub to wash off all that grime—especially if they have had to take the subway!

Throughout the ages, loving owners have found washing their dogs therapeutic. The first thing Queen Victoria did after her coronation was rush back to the palace and shampoo her beloved dog, Dash. And the German Kaiser, when he heard war had been declared, "retired to his cabin and scrubbed the dachshunds."

Poppy's mistress is no exception. She did however have the temerity to shampoo Poppy with wool wash. "If it leaves my cashmere sweaters soft and silky, it will do the same for your fur," she used to say. The indignity of it. Fortunately, one afternoon, Poppy was relaxing in front of the television, when Oprah Winfrey, clearly a human of discernment, recommended a luxury canine shampoo containing aloe vera. Since the switch, Poppy's fur has never looked silkier. Loulou couldn't believe it when Poppy told her about the wool wash—she's never shampooed in anything other than designer dog products.

ABOVE: *Poppy may like sophisticated luxury shampoos, but beneath that cosmopolitan exterior is a dog who really loves to play with her favorite yellow bath toy.*

LEFT: *Loulou adores bath times but, coming from the heat of Mexico, she can't help feeling a little chilly when she gets out. She likes nothing better than to get toasty warm in a stylish bathrobe with a pretty pink check trim.*

LEFT: *Elvis the Bedlington Terrier is pretty in pink. But it's the hand-stitched flowers that truly make this outfit. In gorgeous bright colors, they create opportunities for coordinating accessories—a yellow lead, a blue bow, or perhaps pink painted nails. In addition, they reflect today's 60s fashion revival and the heady days of flower-power.*

BEDROOM CHIC

A girl's boudoir is her haven, a special space where she can powder her nose and pamper herself by trying on all her new clothes.

Elvis (shown on the left) loves to relax in her bedroom, but she always stays style-conscious—her pink jumper ensures that the moment she steps onto the street, she's at ease among the canine fashionistas.

BELOW: Poppy's wardrobe is bursting with outfits that are perfect for her busy city lifestyle, from a night at the opera to a business lunch in Manhattan.

STREET STYLE

As every cool canine knows, it doesn't matter what the designers say—the really great trends emerge from the street. And, with so many different styles of clothes around nowadays, every canine can be a fashion pioneer. Great street looks come from mixing retro with modern, and customizing and mixing unusual items. The more items a dog has in his wardrobe, the more original his street style can be. Before you know it, he'll be an urban trendsetter—he might even feature in one of the street-style blogs that are taking over the web.

LEFT: *Tallulah wears a black parka with white fur trim. Parkas were all the rage with mods in the 60s, so if Tallulah wants to go really retro, she'd better get her owner to take her places by scooter.*

BRING ON THE BLING!

Picture the scene: gray, wintry skies and drizzle. The temperature is dropping. Yet for the fashion-conscious canine it's the perfect excuse to strut her stuff in cuddly, colorful jumpers, and get out her vanity case full of sassy sparkle. In short, it's time to BRING ON THE BLING!

Here, Chanel the Shi-tzu wears a fabulous and vibrant shade of turquoise that sets off the subtle light brown and cream shades of her long coat. But not all fur colors can get away with this. The deep, glossy copper shades of the Red Setter would instead be gorgeously complemented by a strong green; a black coat would be set off by the color scarlet; and fluffy, soft white curls always look exquisite in a fresh lemon number, preferably in cashmere (remember: texture is important).

The favorite pooches of French kings used to sport collars of pearls and diamonds set on deep red velvet. But who needs diamonds, when crystal bling glitters more brightly than the crown jewels? Custom-made collars with crystal letters can shriek "RICH BITCH" through the mist of a London morning, declare undying support for a sports team, or simply and elegantly state a name.

You've always known your pooch is as individual as you are. Let her make her very own loud, proud and glittering fashion statement to the world.

ABOVE: *Chanel's favorite bowl, is of course, gilt-edged. It's far too glamorous to eat from, so she uses it to show off her toys to her canine visitors.*

BELOW: *This shocking pink lead, with crystal bone detailing, is the perfect match for Chanel's equally bright sweater.*

LEFT: *Chanel is modeling a coordinated sweater and bow. In the past, dogs belonging to the wealthy, the famous, and the chic also wore adorable satin or velvet bows tied just above their paws—divine!*

ABOVE: *What canine could object to wearing a fabulous cable knit sweater? Wool is, after all, just as stretchy and snug as a hoody. But whereas hoody screams "attitude," a hand-knit jumper with designer detailing is the height of understated "class."*

DOGZ ON THE BLOCK

Every pooch likes to look her best, even if she's just taking a stroll to the nearest coffee shop. And you know it's the details that will make her stand out in a crowd.

Here, Laska and Elvis model two very different, but equally stylish forms of outerwear.

On the left, Laska the sporty Spaniel wears knitwear that features a traditional sailor's cable stitch. In navy or dark green, this garment would be perfect for a stroll in the country. In warm peach, it is transformed into an eye-catching urban delight that fits in perfectly with the trend for nautical-style tops. This isn't just a contemporary fashion—the sea has always inspired canine couturiers. When posh dogs from the 19th century accompanied their humans to seaside towns in France, it would have been unthinkable for them not to be wearing dashing sailor suits.

RIGHT: *Parkas are all the rage among humans and canines alike. Elvis the Bedlington Terrier wears traditional green with a colorful silky orange lining that lights up her eyes. The detachable hood and legs ensure she doesn't overheat when her owner stops off for a latte on the way home.*

HOODIES RULE

Despite their diminutive size and appealing dark eyes, Pugs are tough, brave guys. In the 19th century huge voracious rats were everywhere—and the important job of rat catching was often given to Pugs. A Pug is a dog with attitude—their Latin motto is *multum in parvo*, meaning a whole lot of dog in a little package.

And what has more street attitude than a hoodie?

Here, svelte black-furred Louis wears a striking red, yellow, and brown designer hoodie. It's perfect for those chilly winter days, and no one is going to mess with him in the park. Unable to resist a bit of bling,

Louis also wears a color coordinated red and white crystal collar.

Zucchi, his companion, knows that he is of too mature a disposition to wear a youthful hoodie, but maintains his pug toughness by wearing a butch sports vest.

Jack, the Jack Russell, adores hoodies too. Jack Russells are the cheekiest dogs on the block. (Remember Martin Crane's Eddie in the long-running sitcom *Frasier*?) And they're totally fearless too. Would Jack run when that 50-kilo Akita is coming his way? Never! Jack reckons hoodies represent his sassy spirit perfectly.

LEFT: *As he likes to run and gambol at every opportunity, Jack likes lightweight, sporty outfits. This purple-and-white striped cotton hoodie, adorned with a cute drawstring treat sack, suits his lifestyle to perfection.*

RIGHT: *Louis poses for the camera while Zucchi relaxes.*

URBAN ATTITUDE: CAMO & DENIM

Elmo is a gorgeous creamy Lhasa Apso whose ancestors came from exotic Tibet. These feisty canines were the faithful guardians of isolated monasteries of Tibet 3,000 years ago, so it's appropriate that today, Elmo has chosen to model an ultra-sharp camouflage jacket. But camo is more than just a uniform that signals top dog, it's an essential component of any urban pup's wardrobe. Since Ralph Lauren introduced his people's military line ten years ago, camo has passed from fashion fad into solid style. This season, look out for camo in the very un-camo shades of red and pink. It looks fab on dark-furred dogs.

Another essential look for the edgy urban dog is denim. Once upon a time, denim was hardy workwear and Levis reigned supreme. Nowadays every designer from Prada to Marc Jacobs wants to put their name on a pair.

RIGHT: *In warm weather, when no canine wants to wear a jacket, Louis (right) remains stylish by sporting a denim bandana with mouthwatering bone motif. Zucchi's green leather collar with brass bones strikes a military note and blends in perfectly with his summer camo bandana.*

LEFT AND BELOW: *Note the strategically placed military badges that make Elmo's jacket the height of camo chic. Where extras are concerned, less is more. Elmo's jacket gets it just right.*

LEFT: *Poppy's denim three-piece, created by canine couturier, Louis Dog, is perfect for any function, smart or casual. The cute frill skirt with heart fabric detail flounces prettily; the jacket can be taken off to reveal a heart fabric T, with lace trim.*

It isn't just jeans though that designers are creating. Everything from urban streetwear to haute couture can look simply sublime in denim. As French designer Leraci Girbaud says: "Putting denim into fashion adds a whole new life to it."

Couture-conscious canines couldn't agree more.

ABOVE & RIGHT: *Ollie has chosen to pair his cool denim jacket with red shoes for a touch of formality.*

25

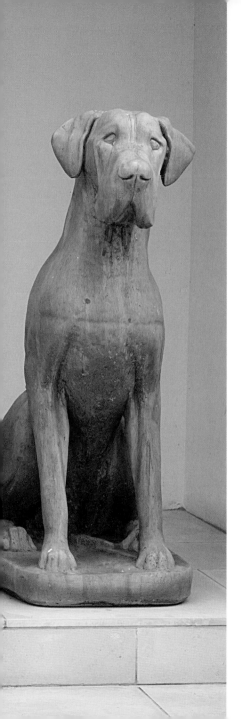

IN THE
COUNTRY

All dogs from the tiniest, most fragile Chihuahua to the greatest Great Dane have as their ancestor the wild intelligent wolf, who even now roams the vast spaces of Yellowstone Park and once padded through the dense oak forests of England.

The countryside is deep in the genes of even the most urban of canines. To the country dog the enticing smell of rabbit hanging in the crisp morning air cannot—and must not—be resisted. The chase is on. But what to wear? Aquascutum check jacket? Camouflage? Or simply *au naturel*?

There's also the constant round of cocktail parties to think about. It can be *so* demanding on the wardrobe: conservative to fit in, or sassy to get noticed? Plus there are the endless games such as tennis tournaments and croquet matches, each with exacting sartorial demands.

Time to go walkies through a fashion minefield.

LEFT: *Flanked by a stone statue of a venerable ancestor, Great Danes Digby, Dylan, and Boris await guests to their vast country estate.*

TO THE MANOR BORN

Spaniels just love the country. They were born and bred in it, and Laska is no exception. Sometimes even the most urban of pooches longs to brave the elements: to frolic in the New York snow, to romp through the rain on a windswept moor, or to splash through delightfully muddy puddles.

After a long run, and lots of fun retrieving balls from muddy ponds, it's time to come home and relax. It's winter, and Beryl the Giant Munsterlander feels quite chilly after her outdoor jaunt. After the obligatory soak in a perfumed bubble bath, she chooses to wear her toasty warm red hoodie.

Time to dream of snuggling up at the fireside as the night draws in.

LEFT: *Laska, in a fitting tribute to his professional cousins (who stealthily retrieved shot ducks for a living), wears a showerproof camouflage outfit with matching hood.*

RIGHT: *Beryl looks adorable in scarlet, and the butch, sporty fleece-style hoodie complements her outdoors personality perfectly.*

PASTORAL POOCHES

Ella, a gorgeous Italian Spinone, comes from a long line of gun dogs, and is at her ease in the country, as is her companion, Lily, the Dachshund.

For chasing rabbits, or just racing through the fields to scatter wood pigeons, they both choose to wear the subtle brown and cream checks of that classic arbiter of British style, Aquascutum.

The British weather is famous for its unpredictability, and in fall and winter Ella and Lily wouldn't dream of going out without their trusty jackets. They even pack them when visiting friends in faraway rural Idaho and snowbound Alaska—for they know that fine country style will always be appreciated.

BELOW: *Ella and Lily just adore their matching jackets. They're essential for country rambles with their master and mistress.*

Summer is a romantic Chihuahua-Pekingese cross whose usual haunt is London's Knightsbridge. Excited at being invited to the country, she rushed off to her favorite designer for advice. "You need camo— it's perfect for walking in nature," he declared. "Whatever *that* is," he muttered under his breath. Now if only Summer had unwrapped the gift-wrapped package before setting off...

Her expression when she saw the bright scarlet trim was priceless. Rabbits and squirrels can spot her a mile away. Not the effect she had hoped for!

COUNTRY PURSUITS

Wimbledon and the US Open bring an annual flurry of enthusiasm for tennis. On both sides of the pond, creaking cupboards are opened, racquets dusted down, and large supplies of tennis balls purchased. Naturally, the country-house set from Gloucestershire to the Hamptons throw lavish tennis parties.

For the discerning canine this is a tricky moment. It's out on court retrieving tennis balls one minute, relaxing on the lawn eating strawberries the next. So... tennis whites or a casual T? Lily gets it just right—stylish enough to hob-nob with other canines after the match, yet practical enough when it comes to finding all those lost balls.

Boo, a Bouvier des Flandres with a tough cattle-herding background, prefers more rough and tumble in his outdoor pursuits. His ideal country afternoon is spent tussling with a football or basketball in a field or garden. His fashion choice—sporty yet trendy—allows him to cut a dash as he frolics.

RIGHT: *The height of tennis chic, Lily wears a fabulous pink tennis ensemble, with white skirt and coordinating pink and white hat with visor.*

BELOW & RIGHT: *This striking blue and white basketball shirt is a must-have for an athletic dog such as Boo.*

"My little dog—a heartbeat at my feet"

REFINED ELEGANCE

Chanel has been invited to the country for the weekend. She knows that when in the country, one must do as country canines do. She has bravely left all her street-style chic at home. Her favorite soft turquoise sweater remains in her wardrobe; her glittering bling gathers dust on her dressing table.

Chanel didn't even visit her extraordinarily expensive groomer before boarding the out-of-town train. Instead, she just gathered up her thick, luxuriant bangs and secured it in a plain band. When running through the undergrowth, Chanel knows it is important to see clearly. The last thing she wants is to trip up and find her country cousins laughing at her. Looking in the mirror, she realises this simple new style emphasizes her melting brown eyes, and wonders if a turquoise rhinestone hairband might be rather fun when she gets back to town. Something bluey-green and sparkly really would bring out the light in her dark eyes, she feels.

For her country stay Chanel wears an understated ribbed sweater in a flattering warm beige—an airforce personnel issue item, bought from the Army Surplus Store—ideal for the great outdoors, not to mention sitting on draughty country window seats.

LEFT: *Chanel, always the perfect guest, has brought her own bed.*

ABOVE: *Wallis, the Hungarian Weimaraner, has chosen a chocolate fleece-lined coat that flatters her exquisite silver-brown fur and complements her soulful eyes.*

COUNTRY CHRISTMAS

The festive season is a crucial part of the fashion calendar. For those in colder locations, there is a careful balance to be struck between comfort and aesthetics as one ventures out carol-singing and present-giving. Fortunately, Christmas is a time when fashion can turn playful. Even humans who usually dress only in discreet black Emporio Armani bring out thick sweaters with white snowflake patterns or grinning Santas at this time of year. Tallulah, a Pug of discernment, who hates feeling chilly, has decided to follow their lead and wear a snug black sweater emblazoned with a reindeer.

Elmo, although anxious to be seasonal, finds wearing a sweater just too darn hot. He does after all have fur thick enough to withstand the winters of high-altitude Tibet. He opts instead for accessories in Christmas colors.

RIGHT: Elmo wears a cheeky red scarf and hat decorated with white spots (he likes the snowflake effect), finished off with large green tassels.

RIGHT: Tallulah hopes the reindeer on her jumper will remind her human that it's G.I.F.T. time.

CITY LIFE

Parisian canines live the metropolitan lifestyle to the full, and have always been welcome in the capital's restaurants. In fact, France is so welcoming to dogs that the English Earl of Bridgewater, concerned for his canines' wellbeing, relocated to Paris where his twelve faithful canines ate with him at table. The pooches were served off silver dishes by their personal servants. The Earl much preferred canine company to that of women.

Today, the five-star Crillon hotel in France has a special menu for dogs. Steak haché is a firm favorite. Or the more bohemian canine can dine in the Marais, chez Le Bouledogue, where the owner, Didier Delor, enthuses that his restaurant is nothing less than a tribute to dogs.

Pooches are also admitted to many chic clubs, fashionable restaurants and exclusive events in Manhattan (even if sometimes, strictly speaking, it is against the rules). And of course, there is a host of glitzy parties, embassy receptions and private views to which the city dog is welcome—providing he or she is wearing the correct attire.

City canines increasingly find themselves in the company of ladies who lunch. Their dog wardrobes must extend not only to sophisticated restaurants, but also to dancing lessons and, in warmer cities, such as Los Angeles, cool pool parties.

LEFT: *Ella loves being the centre of attention. Her collar and leash, in gorgeous fuchsia pink, give her instant star quality in her favorite city restaurants.*

THE EMBASSY RECEPTION

Casper and Mitzy have been summoned to a reception at the Japanese Embassy. In Japan dogs go simply everywhere with their humans. It would be unthinkable for Casper's high-profile diplomatic corps owners to attend such an event without him. And of course, Casper must have an escort. Mitzy accepted his invitation at once. She loves dressing in Japanese clothes. So feminine, so exotic! Plus she knows the dogs' dinner is bound to be super-gourmet.

Chic Japanese designers make the kimono their signature item, and Casper's human has sent away for the authentic articles. Casper, however, has drawn the line at being sent to the pet salon. He read about a dog in Japan being given a mohawk cut, and knows hairdressers can get carried away. Mitzy, however, has insisted on a shampoo and blow out. She doesn't want her fur looking anything less than gleaming.

ABOVE LEFT: *Mitzy loves this kimono, which features chrysanthemums, the Japanese Emperor's flower. She takes it off only when Casper* promises *to give it to her for keeps.*

LEFT: *Casper wears a thoroughly masculine kimono in sophisticated dark blue. The skirt comes decorated with traditional oriental motifs.*

FAR LEFT: *Loulou never slouches. Even when home alone, she likes to be glamorous. Here she wears a fabulous black and red Japanese kimono, with a striking orange bow with pink detail flowers.*

IT'S PARTY TIME FOR GIRLS!

For the city socialite, it's always party time. And Gigi just loves to party. Her wardrobe is full to bursting with dresses for every occasion.

Gigi advises that pastels are the most flattering look for the white-coated canine. Personally, she is partial to powder pink and blue, but says that a deep sumptuous scarlet can look stunning too.

She suggests dark-brown pooches go for more vibrant shades: buttercup yellow or deep aquamarine; while those with a reddish or ginger cast to their fur will look divine in greens and purples.

ABOVE: *Mitzy wears the prettiest ballet tutu in class and holds her luxuriant bangs back with a diamanté bow clip. She doesn't want to trip up in the middle of Swan Lake.*

LEFT: *With her clipped paws, Gigi appears as if she is standing tippie toe in tiny pointed bootee-slippers. A frilly confection, such as this gorgeous blue skirt, lends Gigi a feeling of height and elegance.*

ABOVE: *Gigi says that gold flatters any fur color, but it's important that accessories such as handbags and leashes are gold too.*

PARK LIFE

The stamping ground of the city dog is the park. This is where the style-conscious pooch can strut her stuff and show off her latest outfit. The park is also the place to flaunt skateboarding skills.

Summer, although she looks like choco dog treats wouldn't melt in her mouth, simply adores skateboarding and gives those big boy dobermans a skate for their money! She also takes advantage of all the wonderful dance classes the city has to offer.

Elvis has been visiting Los Angeles, where she was amazed at how dazzlingly bright the sun was and the number of her canine pals who had delicious blue pools. Used to dank ponds, Elvis found swimming in Los Angeles a treat, but what she really enjoys is relaxing pool side.

RIGHT: *Abandoning her normally ultra-feminine attire, Summer wears a street-style chocolate brown hoodie, which means she gets respect out there on the skating lot!*

RIGHT: *In the city of the stars, it's more important than ever to be fashionable. Here, Elvis wears retro-style sunglasses—so cool—and matching harness.*

45

VARSITY AND CHEER-LEADER—THE PREPPY LOOK

The preppy sports look first walked off the campus to become one of the most popular fashions of the 1980s.

Preppy is still popular, but today's canny canine knows it must be worn with a nostalgic sense of irony. Pug pals Zucchi and Louis are well past their student days, and it seems unlikely that basketball was Zucchi's favourite sport... but they love striding out in New England style. They know they look and feel snug and comfy. An ideal combo for travel and hanging out at the coffee shop.

Cheerleading first started at Princeton Uni in the 1880s and was originally a boys-only activity. But now, it's girl power that dominates.

Loulou is a great fan of Madonna and Halle Berry, and figures if they got where they are today by starting in the cheerleading squad, then there's no knowing where her new hobby could take her. She also had her head turned by the hit movie *Bring It On*, about a San Diego high-school squad.

ABOVE: *Zucchi certainly looks pug-nacious in his Varsity 33 jacket.*

RIGHT: *Loulou wears her favorite cheerleading outfit. Bright colors make sure she stands out in a crowd, and fabulous red and white striped pumps tell other dogs that, when it comes to the squad, Loulou's serious.*

FAR RIGHT: *Louis makes no pretensions to being sporty. He wears a lovely ivory jacket that emphasizes the rich blackness of his fur.*

46

WEDDINGS

The dog wedding goes back hundreds of years.
Canine marriage in the royal courts of Europe
was not unusual, but it was in Victorian times
that dog nuptials really came into their own.
Ladies of fashion were horrified at the prospect
of their darlings giving way to rampant passion
and mating with a dog of a different breed, or
worse still, a mongrel. So lavish nuptial ceremonies
followed by a supervised honeymoon became all
the rage.

Now, like us, dogs marry for love, and
contemporary designers create conventional and
avant-garde outfits to suit every pocket.

This chapter takes a look at bridalwear and,
just as importantly, what the fashion-conscious
guest should be wearing.

RIGHT: *Summer looks so
demure peaking out from
behind her veil, topped
with sparkly tiara—but
underneath her traditional
white wedding dress she's
wearing a racy powder-blue
garter.*

THE BIG DAY

Chinese-crested Yorkshire Terrier cross, Poppy, and Jack Russell, Jack, have been planning their wedding for months. They have long admired the 1920s wedding arranged by the Maharajah of Junagadh for his favorite white Bull Terrier, Roshanara. Her Golden Retriever bridegroom was met from his train by the maharajah on a fabulous caparisoned elephant and 250 dogs dressed in jeweled brocade coats.

Given that this would be a tough wedding to top, Poppy and Jack are in a quandary. Should they have their ceremony at the Harrods 4th floor wedding chapel with the reception at the Georgian restaurant afterwards, or should they opt for a more rustic celebration in the garden followed by beef-sponge flavored wedding cake and a rib-bone BBQ?

At least they've decided on the nuptial gown. For a long time Poppy toyed with a scarlet and gold dress. So oriental! Her Chinese mother would have adored it. But in the end, Yorkshire pragmatism won the day and Poppy plumped for traditional white.

FAR RIGHT, ABOVE: *Jack, the dashing bridegroom, wears a crisp white dress shirt, large bow tie and formal black jacket—but draws the line at a top hat.*

FAR RIGHT, BELOW: *Here Poppy wears a conventionally adorable gown fashioned in lustrous white fabric topped with snowflake mesh and adorned with pearls and ribbons. A large bow at the back counterbalances her veil. For now, it is flung carelessly over her back, but on the big day, it will modestly cover her face.*

LEFT & ABOVE: *Pale pink looks delicious against white fur. Diamanté collars are simply divine, especially if Poppy chooses heart charms in romantic pink.*

THE BEST DOG

Ollie, a Parson Jack Russell Terrier, is the cousin of the bridegroom. He has the nerve-wracking privilege of being best dog. Ollie has always favored Japanese designers—he's waiting for the day Kenzo brings out a canine collection. Meanwhile, he has decided to go for a classic Japanese smart-but-chic suit by Nahomilly. It's rather formal by Ollie's standards, but he knows that if he looks smart, he will feel confident giving that all-important speech at the reception.

He was—as he admits to close buddies—strongly influenced in his choice by the fact that the suit has nice large pockets, vital for crib notes and keeping the bride's paw ring safe.

Jack's human, at great expense, has taken his lead from the royal courts of Europe, and engaged an Indian jeweler to create a wrought silver paw ring engraved with a heart linking the names "Jack" and "Poppy." If he lost that, Ollie really would be in the dog house!

BELOW *Ollie takes his time dressing for the big day. First, he puts on his shirt with striking horizontal gold striped tie. This complements the amber flecks in his eyes and brings out his individualistic brown face markings. Satisfied, he puts on dark pants.*

BELOW: *A final check in the mirror confirms that Ollie is perfectly attired to perform the best-dog duties that await him.*

ABOVE: *Ollie tries on the suave and perfectly cut blazer and is delighted with the fit.*

WEDDING BELLES

Loulou was ecstatic when Poppy chose her to be bridesmaid. Her sweet yet understated dress means she looks pretty and feminine, but will not commit the fatal blunder of upstaging the bride.

Gigi, a Parisian Poodle, believes that girls should be girls, and the prettier and pinker the fabric, the better. Taking the saying "pink for a girl" to heart, Gigi has artfully colored the fur on her delightfully fluffy ears and above her delicate feet, a matching powder pink. Divine! Those flash bulbs will certainly be popping.

LEFT: *Gigi wears a delightful frilled pink heart skirt with coordinating top.*

LEFT: *Loulou's floral-print dress in crisp white cotton is wrap-style at the back, and beautifully finished with a lavish satin bow.*

RIGHT: *Loulou, bridesmaid and Ollie's darling, strikes a pretty pose to attract his attention. A side view of her dress shows cute, cap sleeves.*

ACCESSORIES

Every dog knows that accessories can make or break an outfit. Choose a collar that clashes with your fur, and it completely ruins your look. Ollie the Parson Jack Russell and Wallis the Weimaraner are more than aware of the fashion faux paws that other dogs make. They used to have a third dinner companion, Steve the Pitbull, but their friendship turned sour when Steve turned up at Spago in a horrendous orange collar that looked terrible against his brown fur. How embarrassing!

Here, Ollie and Wallis show Steve exactly how things should be done. Both dogs are shining examples of immaculate style. They are keen observers of the latest fashions and trends, and know that bright colors are all the rage on the runways of Milan, New York, and Paris this season. They both go for an eye-catching green tone that accentuates their eyes. Ollie, never one to hold back in the fashion stakes, adds a splash of bright pink to his collar. He knows that if he's to impress the lady pooches in the clubs after dinner he needs to stand out from the crowd—unfortunately his dance moves leave a lot to be desired.

LEFT: *Dinner à deux. Not one to put up with second best, Ollie insists that his serving is as generous as Wallis the Weimaraner's.*

OFF THE LEASH!

In the past, dogs couldn't wait to be let off the leash and allowed to run around chasing sticks and digging holes. For today's modern pooch, things couldn't be more different. Take Poppy, for example—she would feel naked without her treasured accessory, and allows only the finest leashes around her slender neck. There is nothing she likes more than a day out shopping with her favorite human, Melody. Poppy shops for leashes, while Melody tries on shoes in the city's chic boutiques. When Poppy came across this black and white harness, she knew she had to have it. She was even prepared to beg. Luckily for Poppy, Melody agreed that the pattern worked fabulously well with her new Manolos. The pair of them couldn't wait to get home and parade their purchases around the local park.

ABOVE: *When going to parties, Elvis the Bedlington Terrier often wears pink or white with diamanté—her very own tribute to Elvis Presley's inimitable style. She accessorizes with a gorgeous leopard-print handbag.*

RIGHT: *Poppy has several racks of leads, and has personally chosen her favorites to show off here.*

LEFT: *Poppy goes for a simple, chic harness-and-lead combo in classic black and white check.*

A FISTFUL OF COLLARS

Zucchi adores his diamanté collar and crown charm. When he goes on holiday, he always packs a selection—they really add something to a plain outfit without shrieking *townie*!

The other collars here are gifts from Zucchi's girlfriend, Candy. She knows how much he loves those glitter collars that sparkle in a rainbow of colors under artificial light. But because Candy likes to see him modeling the very latest designs, she bought him these bright, fun collars in hot colors. Now Zucchi loves these too.

Zucchi knows that sometimes bling just ain't the thing when he wants to chill out a bit. After a hard day's walking there is nothing he likes to do more than put on his cupcake collar, get himself a nice cool bowl of water, stretch out on his extra cozy blanket, and doze off dreaming of chasing cats for a few hours.

RIGHT: *Here Zucchi wears a fabulous aqua crystal triple row collar from Pugs and Kisses with a diamanté crown charm that tells everyone exactly who's top dog.*

LEFT & FAR LEFT: *Sparkling red and black diamanté, blue bling or gorgeous gold and green—Zucchi wears his chosen collars for walks to the shops or a gentle amble in the park, not just for best.*

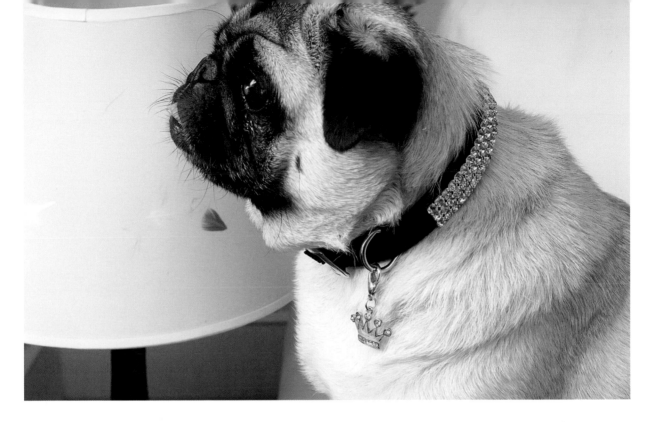

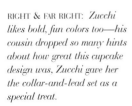

RIGHT & FAR RIGHT: *Zucchi likes bold, fun colors too—his cousin dropped so many hints about how great this cupcake design was, Zucchi gave her the collar-and-lead set as a special treat.*

61

SUPPLIERS

BABIES SF
235 Gough Street
San Francisco
CA 94102
1.888.701.7386
www.babiessf.com

BARK SLOPE
4914 N. Glenwood Avenue
Suite 3
Chicago
IL 60640
1.888.887.9989
www.barkslope.com

DOGGIE FOO FOO
12675 Millview Lane
Charden
OH 44024
www.doggiefoofoo.com

FIFI AND ROMEO
7282 Beverly Boulevard
Los Angeles
CA 90036
323.857.7214
www.fifiandromeo.com

FAB DOG
410 Garibaldi Ave, Suite C
Lodi
NJ 07644
973 472 5555
www.fabdog.com

HANDS 'N' PAWS
3219 East Camelback Road,
#824
Phoenix
AZ 85018
602.522.8300
www.handsnpaws.com

GLAMOUR DOG
2693 Preston Road Suite 1010
Frisco
TX 75034
972.335.1030
www.glamourdog.com

MODERN TAILS
33 Canal Street, Suite 202
New York
NY 10002
www.moderntails.com

THE PAMPERED PUP
119 Datura Street
West Palm Beach
FL 33401
561.833.9948
www.thepamperedpup.com

PAW PALACE
19 W. Front Street
Red Bank
NJ 07701
877.747.9744
www.pawpalaceonline.com

TRIXIE AND PEANUT
23 East 20th Street
New York
NY 10003
212.358.0881
www.trixieandpeanut.com

WAG WEAR
48 East 11th Street
New York
NY 10003
212.673.7210
www.wagwear.com

FETCH
5617 West Boulevard
Vancouver, BC
604.710.2283
www.fetchstore.ca

MY PET BOUTIQUE
155 Dalhousie Street
Unit 1020
Toronto
1.866.469.7387

POOCH CANADA
#882 105-150 Crowfoot
Crescent NW
Calgary, Alberta
403 539-1118
www.pooch.ca

POSH PUP
Orchard Park Shopping Centre
off Highway 97
Kelowna, BC
1.250.861.4PUP
www.poshpup.ca

Elvis tries on a new collar but before she can admire herself, she is distracted from the job in paw, by an open treat jar.

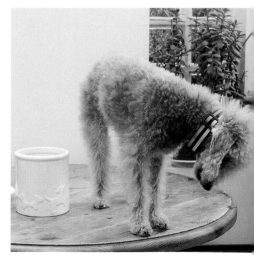

ACKNOWLEDGMENTS

SUPPLIER CREDITS

CREATURE CLOTHES: 22, 38–39, 47 (bed), 60 (bottom right – green collar)

DESIGNER DOGGIE: 50 (right charms), 59 (leads first and third from right), 60 (bottom left – kennel charm), 60 (bottom right – blue & black collars), 61 (top right – crown charm)

DESIGNER DOGGIE/DEAR DOG: 3 (bottom right)

DESIGNER DOGGIE/LE CHIEN: 1, 2, 21 (Louis), 23, 37, 46 (top left & bottom right), 44–45 (bottom), 47 (jacket)

NAHOMILLY: 3 (bottom left), 40–41, 49, 52–53, 55

PET LONDON: 11 (duck toy), 13 (clothes rail), 17 (top right – doughnut toys), 25 (shoes)

PET LONDON/CHACCO: 17 (top right – dog bowl)

PET LONDON/LOUIS DOG: 13 (tutu & heart print shirt), 24, 42

PET LONDON/PET FLYS: 31

PET LONDON/PUPPIA: 3 (top middle), 11 (bathrobe), 13 (striped hoodie), 20, 32, 33, 45 (top right), 51, 58 (bottom left)

PUCHI: 3 (top left), 4, 10, 12, 14, 16, 17 (bottom right), 18, 19, 28, 29, 35, 36, 50 (bottom left), 58 (top right – bag)

PUGS & KISSES: 6–7 (dog treats), 34 (bed), 56 (bowl), 60 (bottom left – collar), 61 (bottom left – blankets), 62–63 (jar)

PUGS & KISSES/BELLA BEAN: 56 (collar), 59 (all leads except third from left, first & third from right), 61 (bottom left – lead), 61 (bottom right – collars), 62–63 (collar)

PUGS & KISSES/GOOBY: 21 (Zucchi),

PUGS & KISSES/HAMPTON REFLECTOR: 59 (lead third from left)

PUGS & KISSES/LULU PINK: 6–7 (red top)

PUGS & KISSES/RUFFDOG: 34 (top)

SPECIAL THANKS TO:

Lucinda Symons; Melody Lewis and Poppy at Pet London; Dan Griffith and Elmo at Elmo's Wardrobe; Effie Michael and Casper at Designer Doggie; Cosima Pole at Creature Clothes; Candace, Ashley and Nikki, Louis and Zucchi at Pugs & Kisses; Nahomi Noritsuke at Nahomilly; Valerie at Puchi; Dorte Beierholm at Hydrovet; Frank Heggie, Jilly Johnson, Helen Nicholson, Kate Haxell, Jane Furnival, Robin Gurdon, Ambrose and Shu Zuo Uzoziri, Scott Boardman, Sandra Carr, Wendy Thorogood, Cheryl Carson, Linda Barker, Jeremy Scholl.

MODELS

ELMO the Lhasa Apso at Elmo's Star Academy

POPPY the Chinese Crested Yorkshire Terrier cross at Pet London Models

GIGI the Miniature Poodle at Pet London Models

MITZY the Yorkshire Terrier at Pet London Models

LOULOU the long-haired Chihuahua at Pet London Models

SUMMER the Pekingese Chihuahua cross at Pet London Models

ELLA the Italian Spinone

LILY the Dachshund

LOUIS and ZUCCHI, Pugs

JACK the Jack Russell

WALLIS the Weimaraner

BERYL the Giant Munsterlander

LASKA the Springer Spaniel

CHANEL the Lhasa Apso

ELVIS the Bedlington Terrier

OLLIE the Parson Jack Russell

BOO the Bouvier Des Flandres

TALLULAH the Pug

CASPER the Cavalier King Charles Spaniel

DIGBY, DYLAN and BORIS, Great Danes.

LEFT: knitted toy bones from Pet London add tone to any color-matched outfit.